Fluent Reader titles are ideal for children who can confidently read books with a wider vocabulary, and who are beginning to read longer stories by themselves.

Special features:

Full exploration of subject

Richer, more varied vocabu...

Detailed illustrations capture the imagination

Captions offer further explanation

Longer sentences

Ladybird

Educational Consultants: Geraldine Taylor and James Clements
Book Banding Consultant: Kate Ruttle
Subject Consultant: Dr Charlotte Adams

LADYBIRD BOOKS
UK | USA | Canada | Ireland | Australia
India | New Zealand | South Africa

Ladybird Books is part of the Penguin Random House group of companies
whose addresses can be found at global.penguinrandomhouse.com.

www.penguin.co.uk www.puffin.co.uk www.ladybird.co.uk

Penguin Random House UK

First published 2019
This edition published 2024
002

Written by Chris Baker

Illustrations by Chelen Ecija

Printed in Dubai

The authorized representative in the EEA is Penguin Random House Ireland,
Morrison Chambers, 32 Nassau Street, Dublin D02 YH68

A CIP catalogue record for this book is available from the British Library

ISBN: 978-0-241-56371-7

All correspondence to:
Ladybird Books
Penguin Random House Children's
One Embassy Gardens, 8 Viaduct Gardens, London SW11 7BW

Experiment guidance: Adult supervision is required.
Do not drink water used in experiments. Do not eat uncooked rice.
Dispose of rice safely once the experiment is complete.

MIX
Paper | Supporting responsible forestry
FSC www.fsc.org FSC® C018179

Read It Yourself

WATER

Written by Chris Baker
Illustrated by Chelen Ecija

Contents

We must have water

We need water to live. Animals and plants must have water, too. If we had no water, we would have no food or drink.

Plants need water to live.

Animals need water to live.

Water at home

As well as needing water to drink, we need water for washing, and for many other things.

Here are some of the other things we do with water.

Electricity from water

Water has power. It can make a rotor turn.

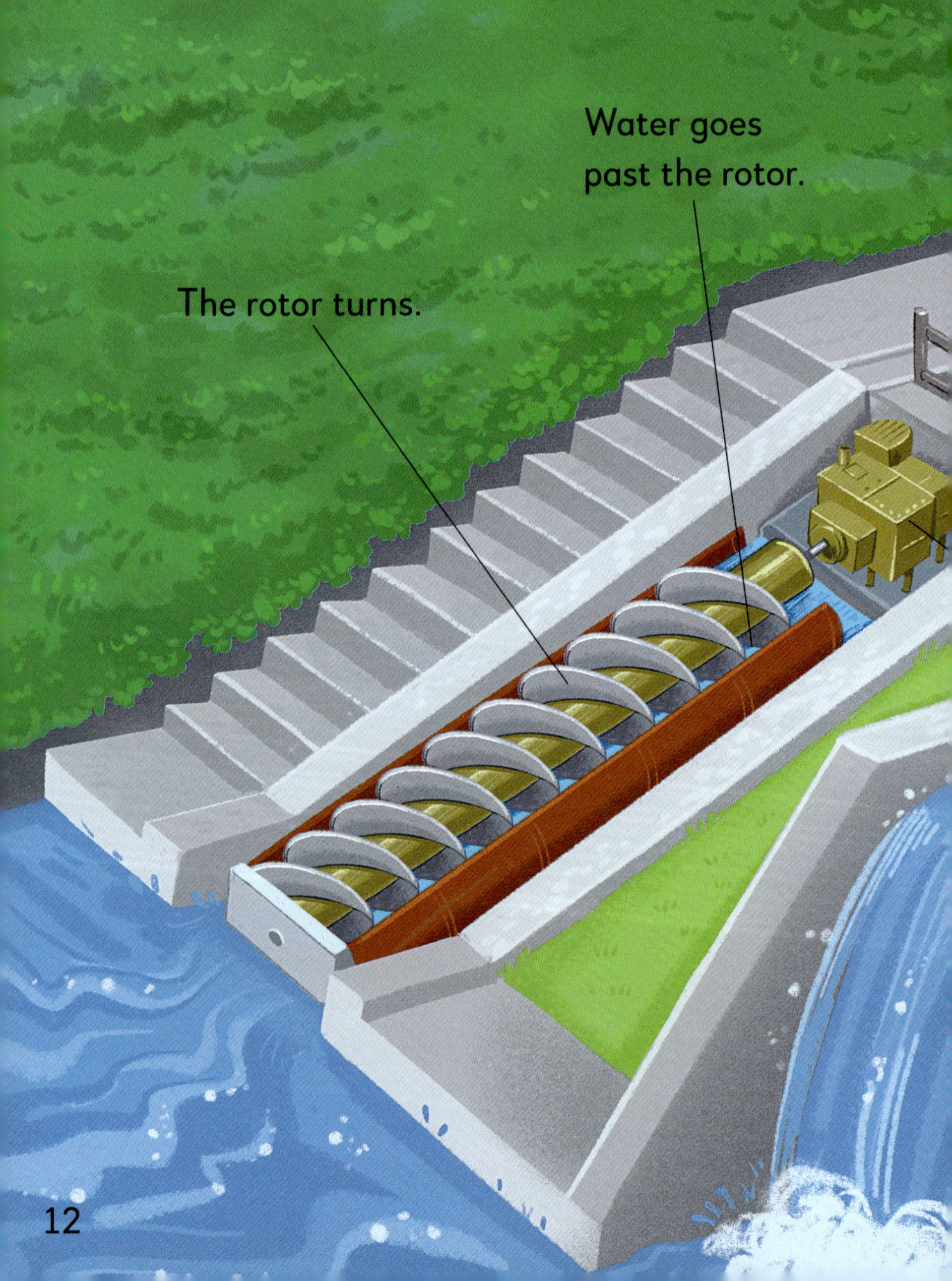

When the rotor turns,
the power makes electricity.

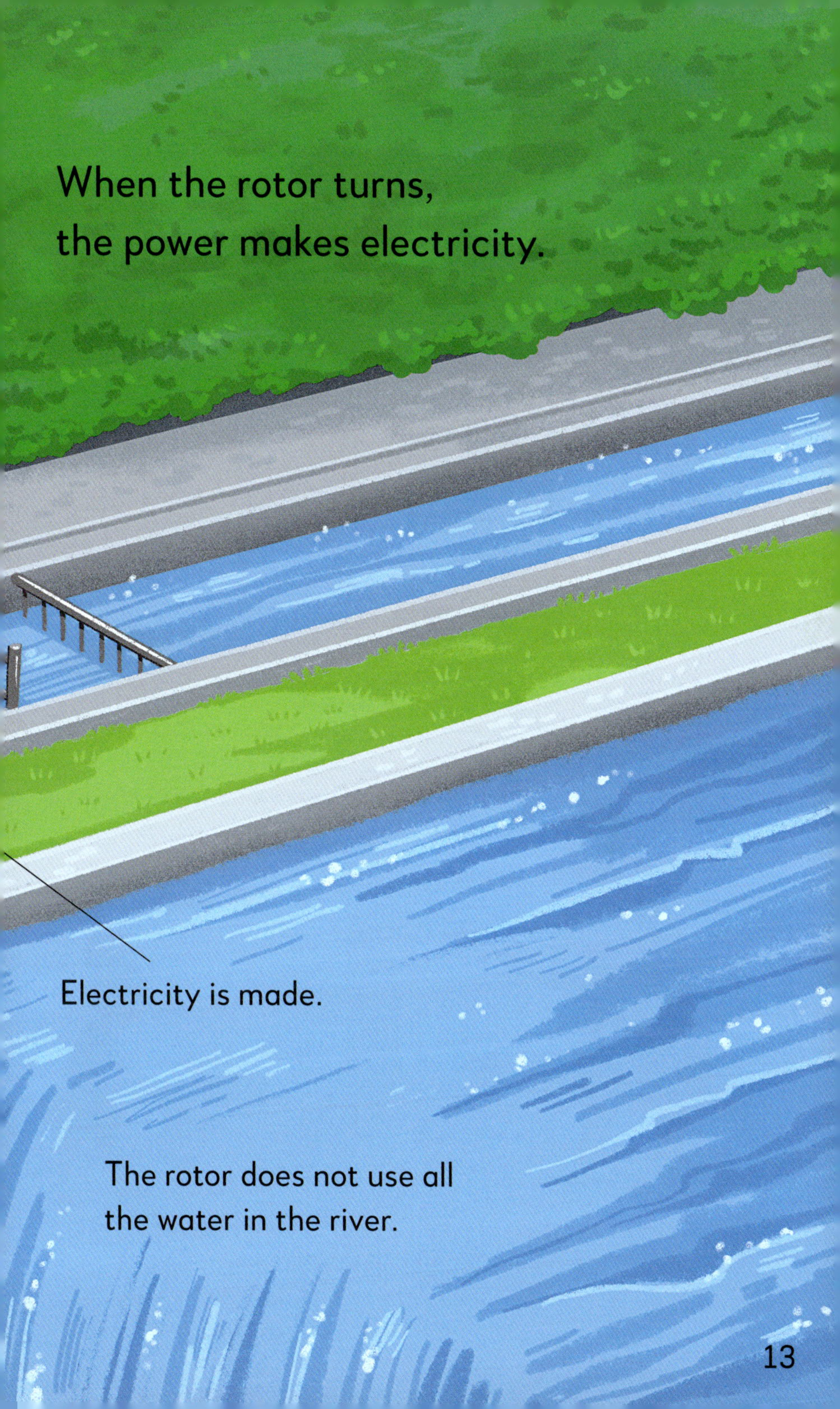

The rotor does not use all
the water in the river.

Where does water come from?

Everyone needs water, and there are many ways to collect it.

There are many ways to get water.

The water cycle

If we want to know where water comes from, we must know about the water cycle.

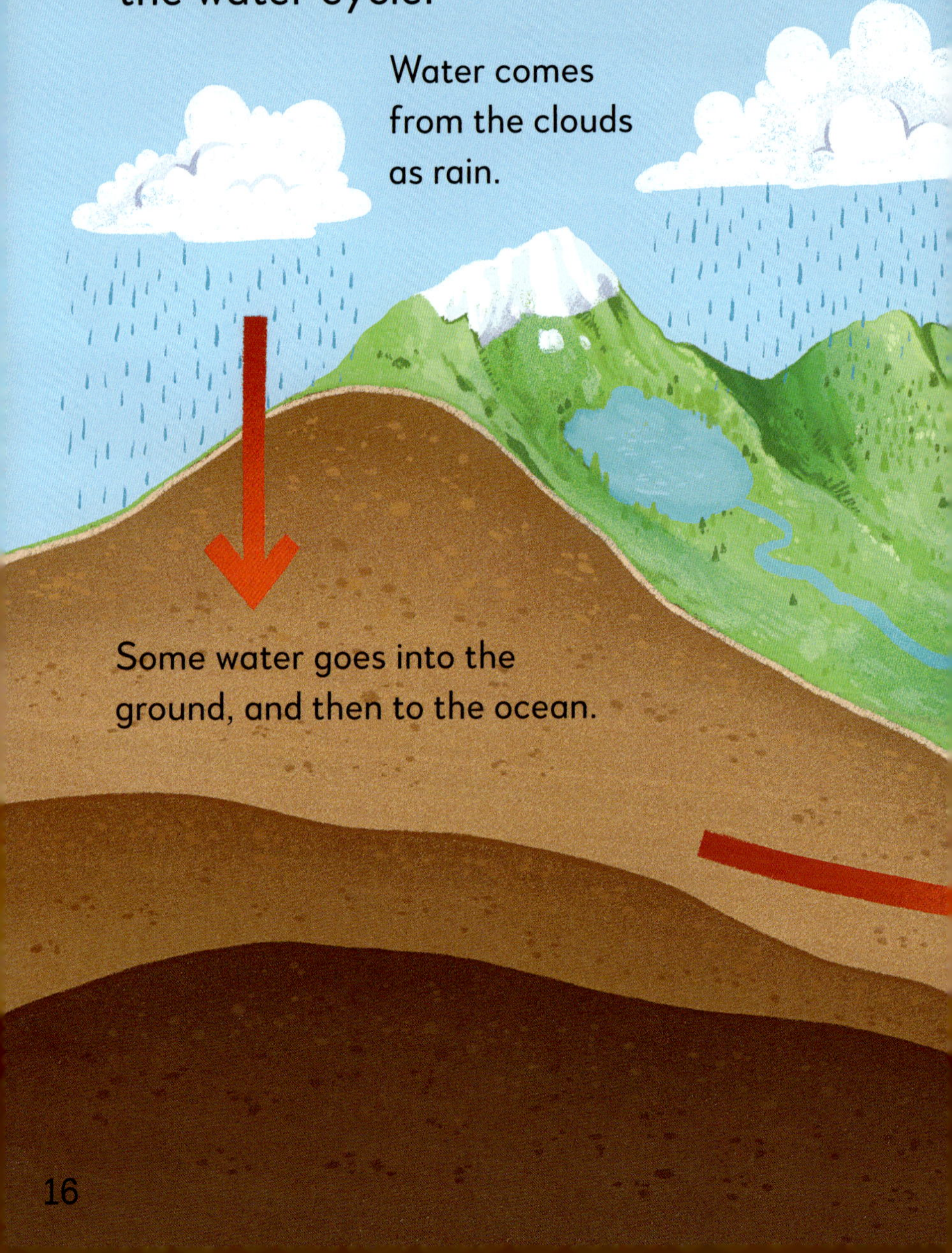

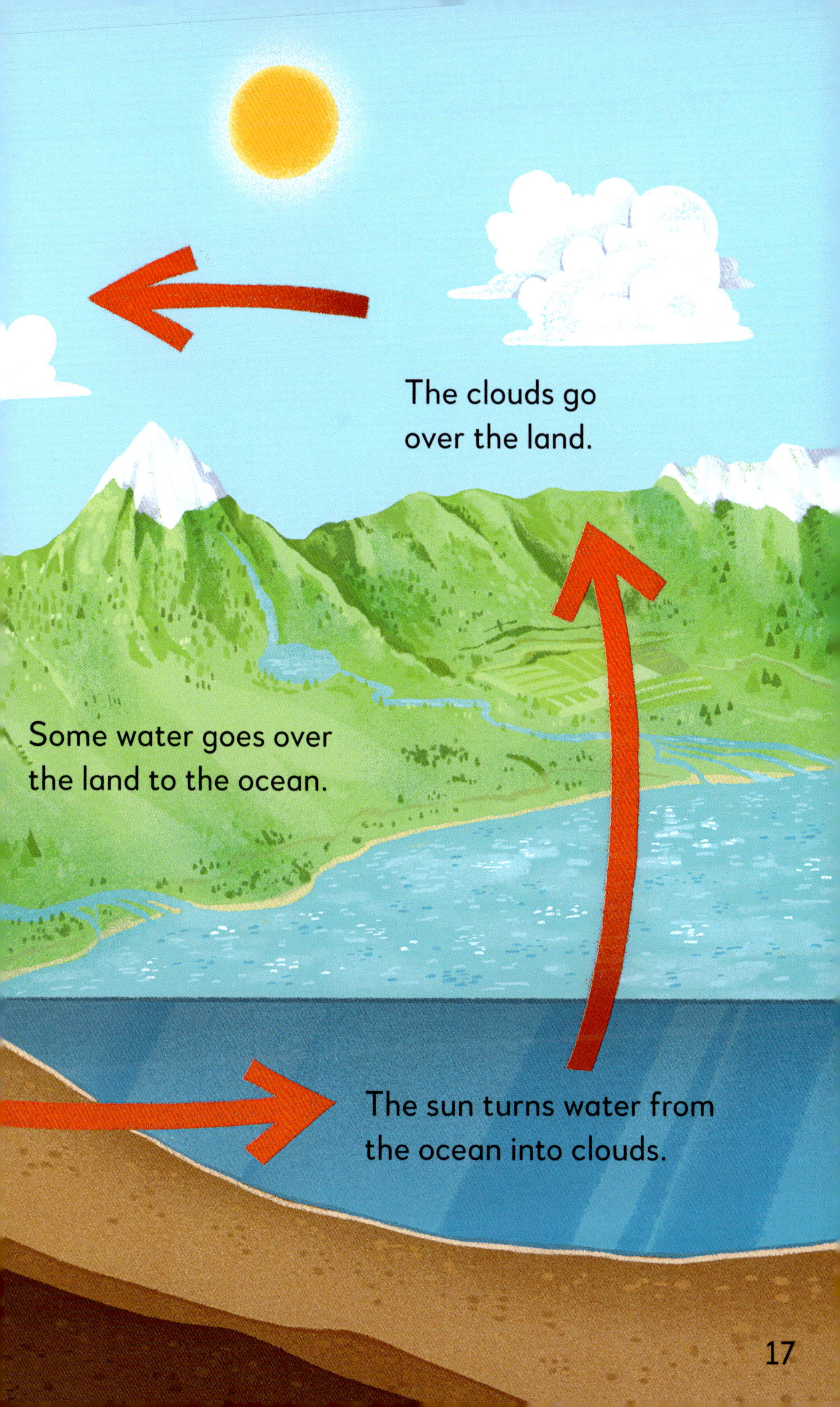

The clouds go over the land.

Some water goes over the land to the ocean.

The sun turns water from the ocean into clouds.

Water we can't use

Most of the water in the world is in the ocean. We can't drink water from the ocean because it is salty.

People by the ocean must drink fresh water from home.

We can only use water from parts of the water cycle where the water is fresh.

Water stores

People have to store enough water that is not salty. It must be stored where it can be used by everyone.

This reservoir is like a very big water barrel. It can store water and make electricity, too!

Freshwater treatment

Water in our taps can come from rivers, a reservoir or under the ground. The water is cleaned to make it safe to drink.

Water gets cleaned at the freshwater treatment plant.

No water!

Sometimes there is a water emergency, and there is not enough water for everyone. Then, people must use as little water as they can.

Sometimes, the taps are turned off, and people must collect water in big bottles.

How we can save water

There are things everyone can do to save water and not have a water emergency.

Use a barrel to collect rainwater.

Use rainwater in the garden.

Turn off the taps.

Don't use too much water for washing.

Everyone can help to save water.

Dirty water

Sometimes, we make the water dirty. This dirty water is now part of the water cycle.

This can cause problems if we don’t make the water clean and safe again.

Dirt and rubbish get into the water.

Water pollution

When things get into the water that should not be there, they cause water pollution.

Rubbish, dirt, chemicals and germs can all cause water pollution. It is a big problem.

What water-pollution problems can you see here?

Waterborne diseases

Waterborne diseases are diseases people get from wastewater that has germs in it.

There is a problem with this toilet.
Germs should not be getting into the water.

People can get sick when they use the dirty water.

Wastewater treatment

When we have used water, it is cleaned again. This prevents waterborne diseases and pollution.

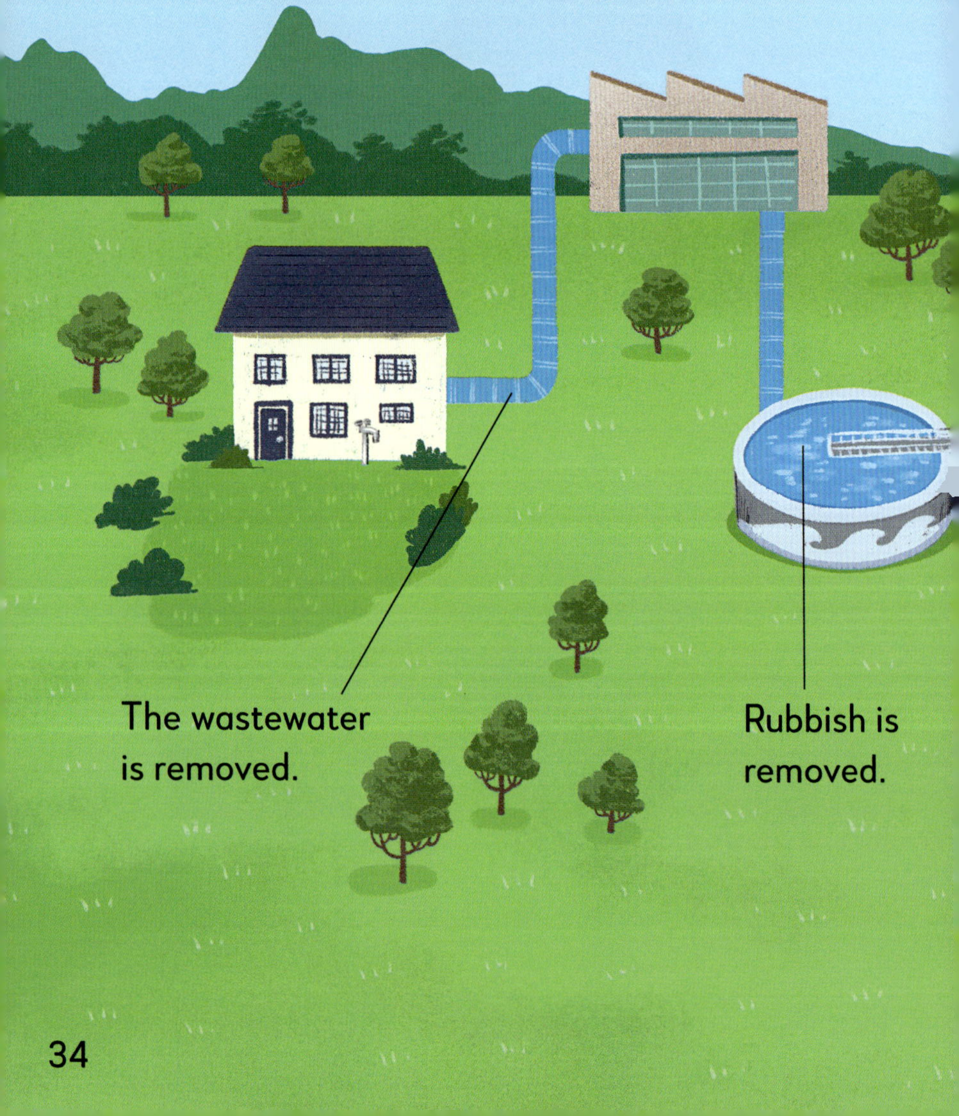

The water can then go into the rivers again.

Plastic pollution

We can prevent water pollution by recycling plastic, and by not putting things down the toilet.

Rubbish is put down the toilet.

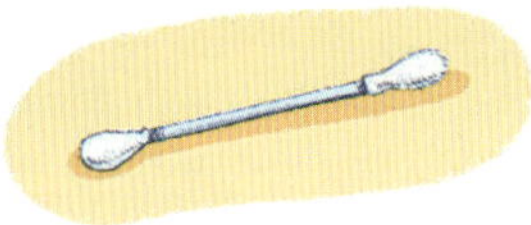

Rubbish turns into little pieces.

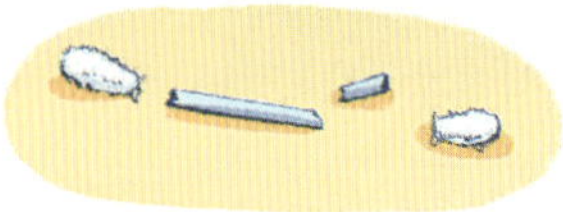

Little pieces get into rivers and the ocean.

The little pieces can make animals sick.

Some things do not have
to be made of plastic.

How to clean the ocean

What can we do about the plastic rubbish that is in the ocean now?

People can make a barrier to remove it.

This floating barrier helps to clean up!

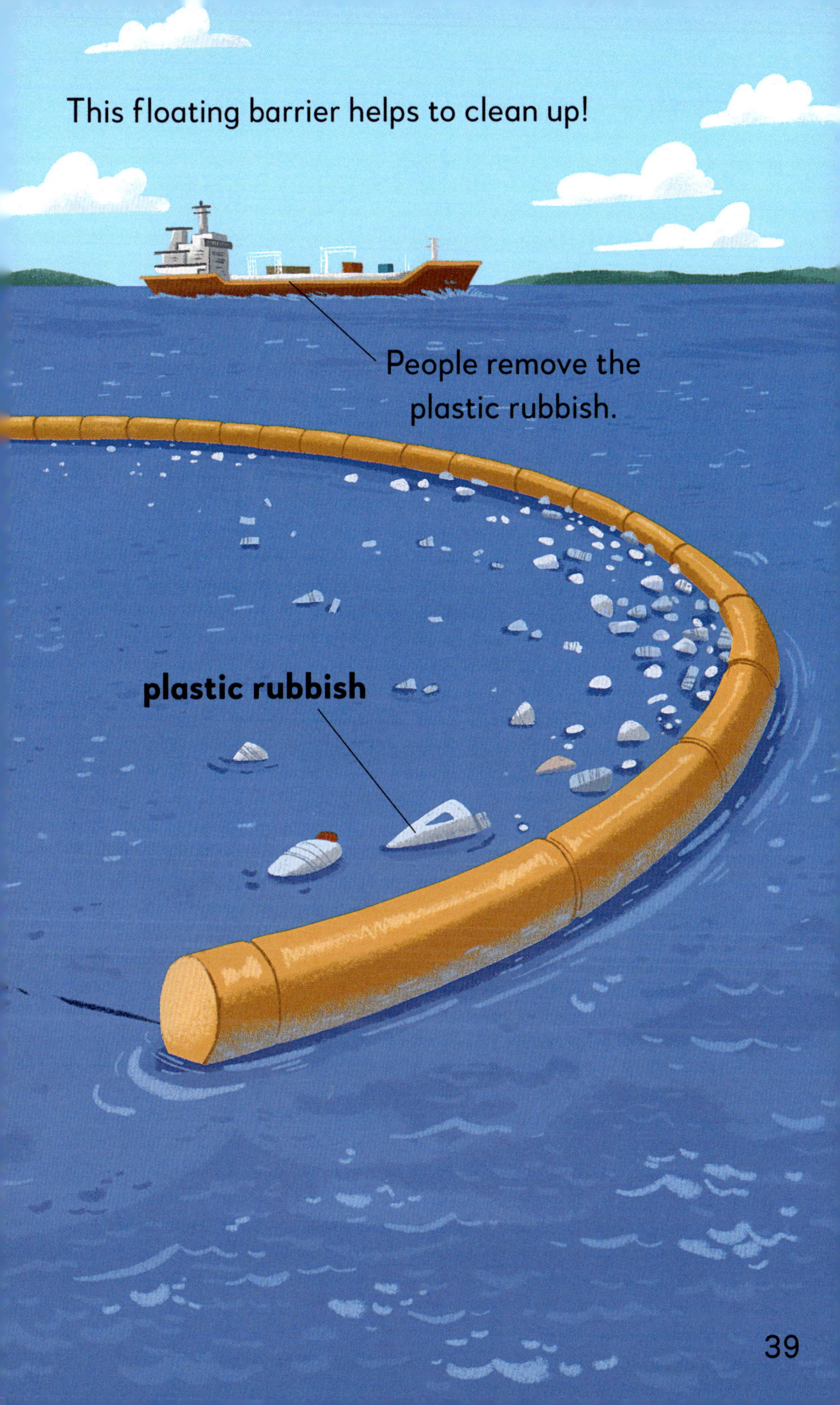

Make a model water cycle

Now, it's your go! Put salty water in a bowl like this.

This is a model water cycle!
Put it in the sun.

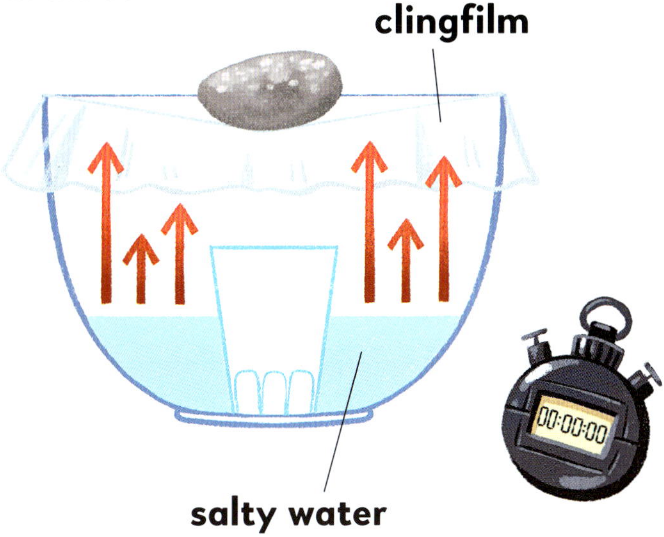

Make a model water treatment plant

Water treatment plants use filters to remove rubbish. Put rice in some water to be the rubbish – then clean it up with a filter.

rice
water

Picture glossary

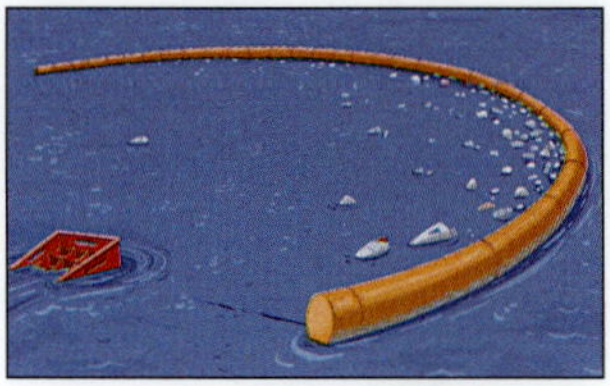

barrier

emergency

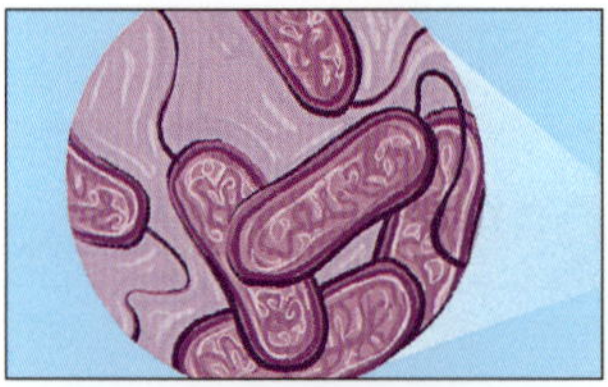

germs

ocean

pollution

rainwater

reservoir

rotor

water barrel

water cycle

water tank

water treatment

Index